Contents

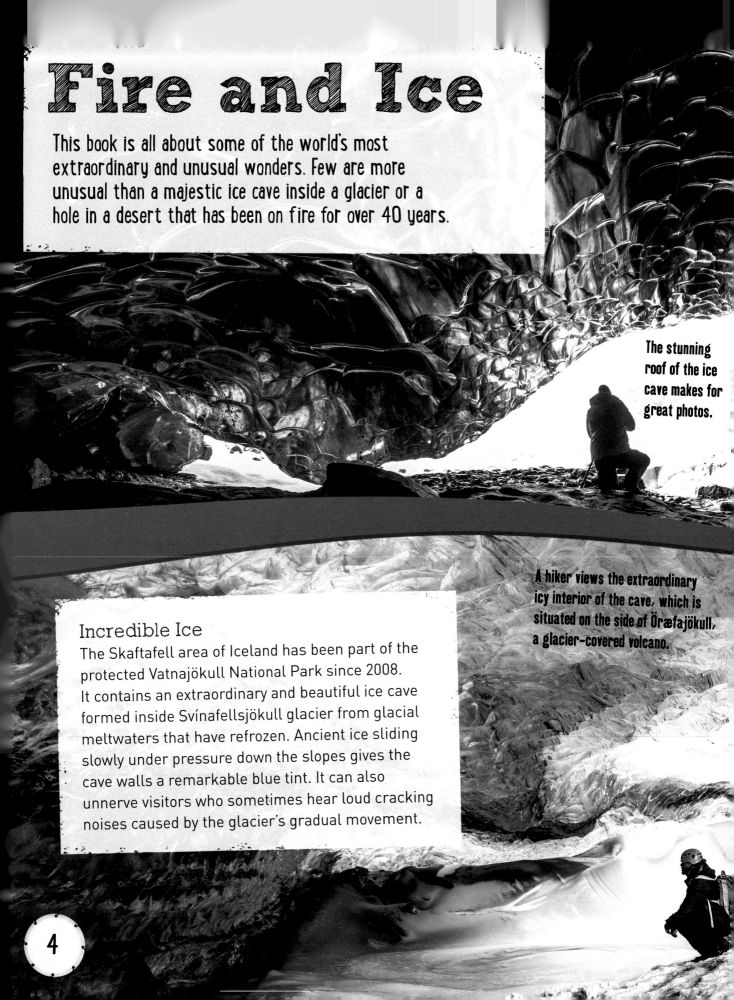

Fire and Ice

This book is all about some of the world's most extraordinary and unusual wonders. Few are more unusual than a majestic ice cave inside a glacier or a hole in a desert that has been on fire for over 40 years.

The stunning roof of the ice cave makes for great photos.

A hiker views the extraordinary icy interior of the cave, which is situated on the side of Öræfajökull, a glacier-covered volcano.

Incredible Ice

The Skaftafell area of Iceland has been part of the protected Vatnajökull National Park since 2008. It contains an extraordinary and beautiful ice cave formed inside Svínafellsjökull glacier from glacial meltwaters that have refrozen. Ancient ice sliding slowly under pressure down the slopes gives the cave walls a remarkable blue tint. It can also unnerve visitors who sometimes hear loud cracking noises caused by the glacier's gradual movement.

Worldwide
Wonders

UNUSUAL WONDERS

Clive Gifford

WAYLAND

Published in paperback in Great Britain in 2018 by Wayland

Copyright © Wayland, 2016

Editor: Nicola Edwards
Design: Peter Clayman

ISBN: 978 0 7502 9871 1

10 9 8 7 6 5 4 3 2 1

Wayland, an imprint of
Hachette Children's Group
Part of Hodder and Stoughton
Carmelite House
50 Victoria Embankment
London EC4Y 0DZ

An Hachette UK Company
www.hachette.co.uk
www.hachettechildrens.co.uk

Printed and bound in China

Picture acknowledgements: All images and graphic elements courtesy of Shutterstock
except p5t and b, 28br Wikimedia Commons; pp14b, 18b, 20 and 25b Getty images;
p26t Corbis

Every attempt has been made to clear copyright. Should there be any
inadvertent omission, please apply to the publisher for rectification.

The website addresses (URLs) included in this book were valid at the time of
going to press. However, it is possible that contents or addresses may have
changed since the publication of this book. No responsibility for any such
changes can be accepted by either the author or the Publisher.

It's a Gas

Turkmenistan is home to one of the world's largest natural gas fields, mostly located in the Karakum Desert. Oil prospectors from the Soviet Union were working in the field in 1971 when an old underground cavern collapsed and their drilling equipment disappeared into a giant hole. Fearing natural gas leaks might reach nearby towns, the engineers set fire to the gas to burn it all off. It was a process they thought would take weeks but is still continuing today, some 45 years later!

The Darvaza crater is also known as the Door to Hell and the Crater of Fire.

The Door to Hell

The flaming crater is approximately 69m wide and 30m deep and contains thousands of small fires fuelled by natural gas, which make the crater's mud boil and bubble. Named Darvaza Crater, but also known as the Gateway to Hell or Door to Hell, it attracts more than 10,000 tourists per year.

Pockets of gas burn fiercely within the crater.

WOW!

In 2013, Canadian explorer, George Kourounis entered the burning Darvaza Crater in a special flame-proof suit, which protected him from the 1,000°C temperatures inside.

The Chocolate Hills

Bohol is the tenth largest island in the Philippines with an area of 4,821 km^2.
It is famous for its white sand beaches and the tarsier, a rare primate,
but most of all for its awesome collection of symmetrical cone-shaped hills.
These dot the landscape at the centre of the island.

Collections of rounded hillocks do exist elsewhere in the world, but few are as numerous, extensive or all as similarly shaped as Bobol's extraordinary hills.

Humps and Hillocks

The Chocolate Hills number more than 1,260 in total and all are remarkably similar. Most rise between 30m and 50m above the surrounding landscape, with the tallest peaking at 120m. In between the hills on the flatter land beneath, farmers cultivate rice and other crops. The hills are made of limestone covered in topsoil and grass. For most of the year, they look green in colour. During the dry season several species of grass turn a dark brown, giving the hills the chocolate brown colour for which they are named.

Hill Formation

Several local legends tell how the hills were formed. One says they were the work of two giants who fought across the land for days, eventually becoming friends but not clearing up the mess they left behind, which became the hills. Geologists, however, believe that the limestone forming the hills originally came from rock formations underwater. The rocks were forced upwards by movements of the Earth's plates and then eroded by rain and streams to form their smooth, rounded shapes.

Conservation or Exploitation

Despite being protected by the Philippines government as a National Geological Monument in 1988, the hills are under threat. There's a risk of damage from occasional major earthquakes in the region and from human interests in exploiting the hills' limestone rock by quarrying and through expanding tourist operations. Only two hills have been developed into tourist hotels and resorts as the authorities try to achieve a balance between generating income and preserving the hills for future generations.

The viewing deck of the Chocolate Hills Complex.

WOW!

Sagbayan Peak is a popular viewing point for the Chocolate Hills. This strange place features a butterfly house and a life-size model of a two-legged predatory dinosaur!

Tsingy de Bemaraha

Deep in the western region of the Indian Ocean island of Madagascar lies a strange area made up of large numbers of 60–90m-tall spiky rock towers. Visitors who manage the tricky journey here are rewarded with a view of the world's largest stone forest.

Trees and bushes grow among the jagged limestone spires of this unusual stone forest.

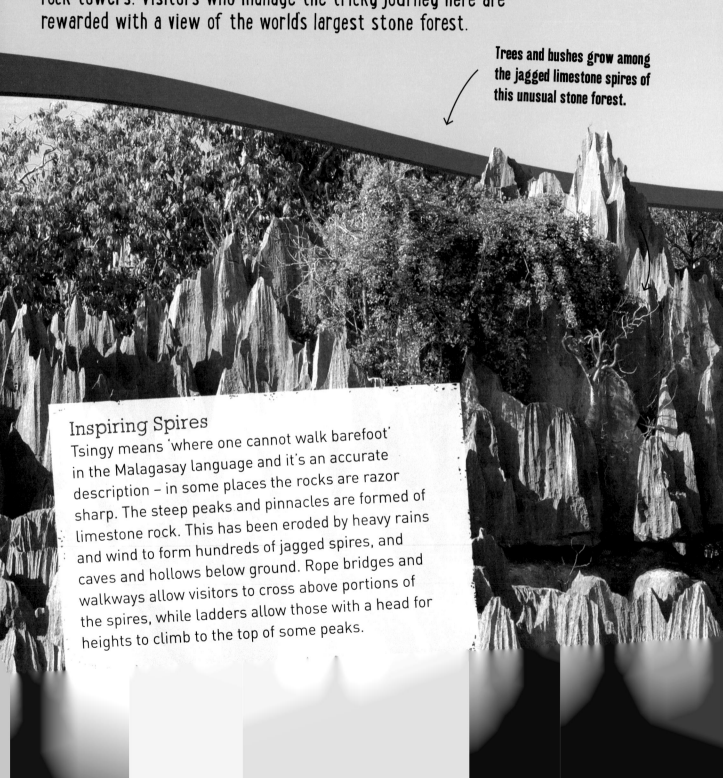

Inspiring Spires

Tsingy means 'where one cannot walk barefoot' in the Malagasay language and it's an accurate description – in some places the rocks are razor sharp. The steep peaks and pinnacles are formed of limestone rock. This has been eroded by heavy rains and wind to form hundreds of jagged spires, and caves and hollows below ground. Rope bridges and walkways allow visitors to cross above portions of the spires, while ladders allow those with a head for heights to climb to the top of some peaks.

WOW!

Tsingy is home to a number of species of chameleon that are among the world's smallest reptiles – some are as tiny as the width of your fingertip.

The ladders, walkways and rope bridges form eight circuits or routes around the area each with a different level of difficulty.

Hostile Home

Despite the hostile rocky conditions, many living things make their home among or close to the peaks. There are 11 different species of lemur, dozens of different birds, including the endangered and rare Madagascar fish eagle, and more than 40 species of reptile. Tsingy became a UNESCO World Heritage site in 1990 and is split into two protected areas – a National Park and the Tsingy de Bemaraha Strict Nature Reserve.

Colourful robber flies attack and feed on other insects.

Meteora Monasteries

People have lived in caves in parts of the Plain of Thessaly in Greece for thousands of years. Around 650–700 years ago, Christian hermits and monks began living at the top of giant sandstone pillars in the region near the town of Kalambaka. The extraordinary structures that were eventually built on these columns of rock became known as Meteora, which is Greek for 'suspended in the air'.

The Holy Trinity Monastery, perched on a 400m-high rock, was built in the 1470s.

Agios Stefanos Monastery was built in the sixteenth century and has been home to a group of nuns since 1961.

Peak Perfection

The earliest buildings on these 60 million-year-old sandstone peaks were simple living quarters and places of worship carved into the rock, such as St Athanasios Meteorites built in 1340. Over time, more elaborate buildings were created on top of these columns in the toughest possible conditions. There were no staircases or roads up the sheer peaks. Building materials had to be hauled up the steep sides using ropes and baskets made of netting.

Surviving Six

Around 24 monasteries are believed to have been built by the sixteenth century. Some were abandoned while others suffered severe damage during World War II. Six of the monasteries still operate today. Two of these, including the easiest to reach, Agios Stefanos Monastery, are homes for nuns. Perched on top of Platýs Líthos (meaning Broad Rock), 615m above sea level, is the largest monastery, the Great Meteoron. All the Meteora monasteries contain a wealth of religious paintings, manuscripts and ornaments.

WOW!

The Monastery of Varlaam only had a staircase built up to it in 1923, more than 400 years after the building was constructed!

Colourful religious art decorates the Monastery of the Holy Trinity.

Coming into Contact

For centuries the monasteries remained isolated from the outside world. Many used winches to lift supplies up the rocky columns, but have more recently benefited from modern innovations. A funicular cable train ferries supplies to the Agia Triada Monastery, and a bridge, built in 1930, makes it easier for people to access the Rousannou Monastery. Tourists can visit the monasteries, but must observe the religious rules concerning appropriate clothing and behaviour.

The skulls of former monks are kept at the monasteries.

Salar de Uyuni

A giant prehistoric saltwater lake, Lago Minchin, once covered most of south-western Bolivia. When it dried up over 10,000 years ago, it left behind several small lakes and a gigantic salt flat. Called Salar de Uyuni, it is 10,582km^2 in area, making it bigger than some entire countries including Cyprus and Lebanon.

Mirror, Mirror

Found at an altitude of 3,653m, Salar de Uyuni is almost perfectly flat across its giant extent, deviating by no more than a metre. Coupled with clear skies most of the time, its reflective surface acts like a mirror when a thin layer of water covers it, making it great for fun tourist photos. Its large size and flatness is also used by some space satellites to send and bounce signals off to check on their altitude above the planet's surface as they orbit Earth.

Mine's some salt

The salt is more than 10m thick in the centre of the salt flats and approximately 25,000 tonnes of salt are recovered from Salar de Uyuni every year. The salt is mined locally by a worker cooperative. With scientists estimating that Salar de Uyuni contains around 10 billion tonnes of salt, the supply will not be running out anytime soon. The area's other industry is tourism – some 60,000 tourists visit the area every year.

An old steam trains lies rusting near Uyuni. A train line ran here from 1892 until the 1940s.

Salt is scraped from the surface into cone-shaped pyramids and left to dry in the sun before being processed.

WOW!

Salar de Uyuni may contain as much as 30 per cent of all the world's lithium – an important element used in the making of millions of rechargeable batteries.

In the Pink

The flats contain relatively little natural life. The few plants are mostly types of *Echinopsis* cactus, which can grow up to 12m tall, along with some quinoa and thola plants. Wildlife is mostly restricted to birds. In November, Uyuni becomes a riot of pink as three different species of flamingo (and some other birds) flock to the area to breed.

James's flamingos, Chilean flamingos and Andean flamingos are found on the salt flats, feeding mainly on algae and plankton.

Ajanta Caves

Stunning stone work in Cave 26 includes a Buddhist stupa holding religious relics.

In 1819, young British soldier, John Smith, made an extraordinary discovery while on a tiger-hunting trip. Obscured behind heavy undergrowth was a cave full of ancient stone carvings and wall paintings. It turned out to be just one of 29 ancient caves cut into a rock face some 76m above the Waghur River in India's Maharashtra state. The caves had lain hidden for well over 1,000 years.

Tourists visit the cave complex.

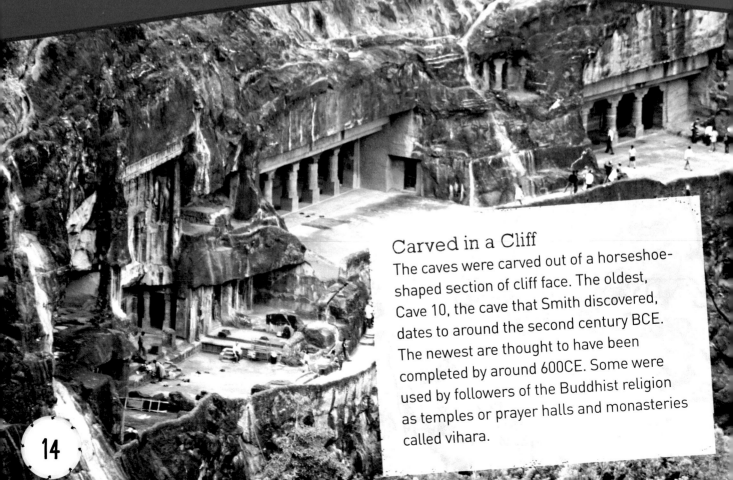

Carved in a Cliff

The caves were carved out of a horseshoe-shaped section of cliff face. The oldest, Cave 10, the cave that Smith discovered, dates to around the second century BCE. The newest are thought to have been completed by around 600CE. Some were used by followers of the Buddhist religion as temples or prayer halls and monasteries called vihara.

Astonishing Art

The caves contain some amazing architecture, with inner walls, columns, altars and stone galleries all chiselled out of the cliff rock. The temples and prayer halls are decorated in incredible detail. Hundreds of carvings and sculptures of deities, animals and figures as well as extraordinarily detailed paintings make up one of the biggest collections of early Indian art ever found. The paintings were made by grinding up minerals such as yellow ochre and lapis lazuli into a powder and mixing it with vegetable gum and glue made from the bones of animals.

WOW!

Two early attempts to make copies of the Ajanta cave paintings ended in disaster. The first, by Robert Gill, mostly perished in a London fire in 1866, while Japanese artist Arai Kampō's copies were destroyed in a giant earthquake in 1923.

Avalokitesvara is a Buddhist figure known for compassion.

Threats and Replicas

The Ajanta's architectural treasures are under threat in several ways – from pollution to tree growth, where roots snake their way through joints in the rock, widening cracks. An increase in visitor numbers has also led to the delicate paintings being damaged. In 2012, four of the caves were closed to tourists by the state tourism authorities. The following year, replicas of these four caves, created by a Mumbai designer along with 150 craftspeople, were opened at the visitor centre 4km from the rock face.

The Wave

The Vermilion Cliffs National Monument is an area of rocky desert on the Arizona-Utah border in the United States. It features many astonishing rock formations made from twisted and eroded layers of sedimentary sandstone rocks. None is more breathtaking and otherworldly than the Wave.

Sandstone Swirls

The Wave is a sort of twisting ravine made up of two troughs, the largest measuring 19m wide and over 35m long. They were formed more than 180 million years ago from giant Jurassic sand dunes that over long periods of time became compacted into rock. The rock was first eroded by water cutting through it, then by wind erosion, which created the formation's sweeping, swirling curves. Different levels of iron oxide in the layers of sand resulted in a rainbow of yellow, pink and red layers that give the Wave its striking, striped colours.

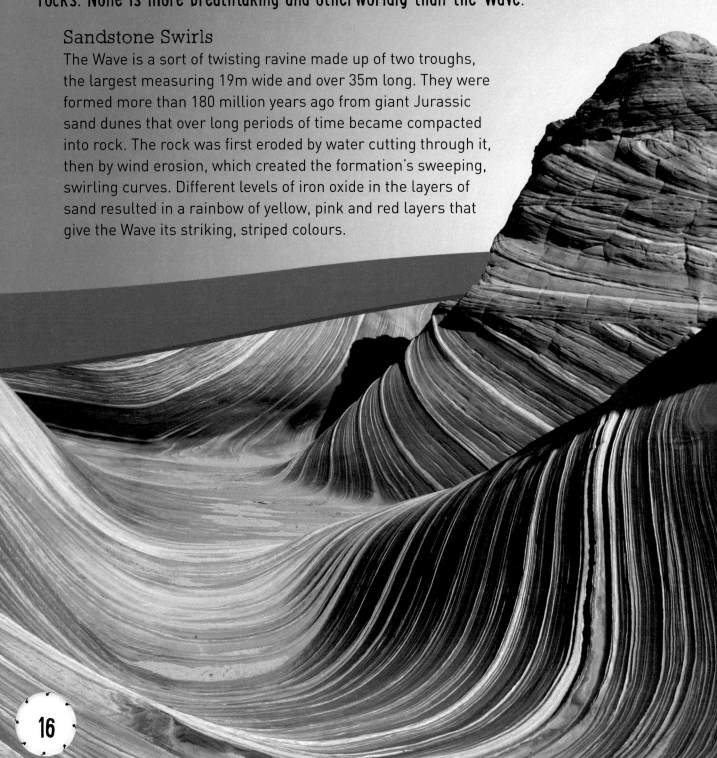

Limiting Lottery

The Wave was first protected in 1984 when it became part of the Paria Canyon-Vermilion Cliffs Wilderness protected area. Today, it is looked after by the Bureau of Land Management who, to preserve the sandstone structures, only issue 20 permits to walk through the Wave each day. Half of these are awarded by a lottery that hikers can enter four months in advance of their trip. Many thousands apply in the hope that they will win a coveted chance to experience the Wave up close.

The Wave's spectacular sandstone ribs and ridges are best viewed on sunny days.

WOW!

Close to the Wave is a group of more than 1,000 dinosaur footprints, some 40cm long, all packed into a small area and made by two and four-legged dinosaurs around 190 million years ago.

Dali Rock, also nicknamed 'the Control Tower'.

Sculpting the Sandstone

The Wave is not the only strange sandstone formation within Vermilion Cliffs. Wind and water erosion of the sandstone has created some extraordinary shapes, including buttes – isolated hills with steep sides – and hoodoos, stone columns formed from eroded softer rock with harder rock on the top. Some of the strange formations have been given atmospheric nicknames, such as the Broken Cathedral and the Totem Pole.

The Boneyard

Close to the town of Tucson, in the US state of Arizona, lies Davis-Monthan Air Force Base. Part of this base is given over to a massive parking lot for military aircraft that are no longer in service. Its official name is the 309th Aerospace Maintenance and Regeneration Group but it is better known as 'The Boneyard'.

Picking the Place

Davis-Monthan Air Force Base was founded shortly after World War I and was named after two pioneering American pilots. Home of the 355th Fighter Wing and other squadrons of operational aircraft, it was chosen in 1946 as the site of a giant storage project. Tucson's low rainfall and low humidity plus its relatively high altitude of 780m all helped to slow down the rusting of steel aircraft parts. In addition, the hard soil at the base made it possible to move the planes without needing to build large numbers of concrete or steel roads and ramps.

An aerial view of part of the Boneyard. As well as the aircraft, the base holds a collection of 700,000 aviation tools and parts.

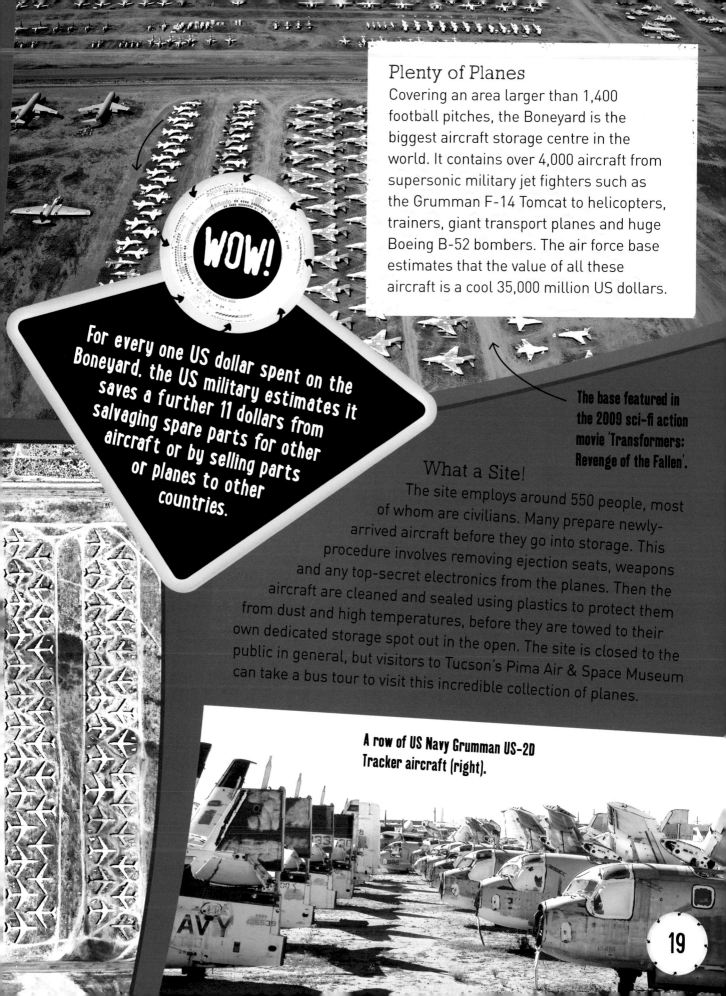

Plenty of Planes

Covering an area larger than 1,400 football pitches, the Boneyard is the biggest aircraft storage centre in the world. It contains over 4,000 aircraft from supersonic military jet fighters such as the Grumman F-14 Tomcat to helicopters, trainers, giant transport planes and huge Boeing B-52 bombers. The air force base estimates that the value of all these aircraft is a cool 35,000 million US dollars.

WOW!

For every one US dollar spent on the Boneyard, the US military estimates it saves a further 11 dollars from salvaging spare parts for other aircraft or by selling parts or planes to other countries.

The base featured in the 2009 sci-fi action movie 'Transformers: Revenge of the Fallen'.

What a Site!

The site employs around 550 people, most of whom are civilians. Many prepare newly-arrived aircraft before they go into storage. This procedure involves removing ejection seats, weapons and any top-secret electronics from the planes. Then the aircraft are cleaned and sealed using plastics to protect them from dust and high temperatures, before they are towed to their own dedicated storage spot out in the open. The site is closed to the public in general, but visitors to Tucson's Pima Air & Space Museum can take a bus tour to visit this incredible collection of planes.

A row of US Navy Grumman US-2D Tracker aircraft (right).

The Cave of Crystals

Crystals often have a length measured in millimetres or centimetres, but 300m below the surface next to lead, zinc and silver mines in Naica, Mexico, lies a cavern that's home to crystals that are seriously super-sized.

Gigantic Gypsum

Discovered in 2000 by two mining brothers, the Cave of Crystals is a horseshoe-shaped limestone cave. With a chamber of hot magma rock several kilometres below the cave, conditions inside are extremely humid (over 90 per cent humidity) and hot, with temperatures reaching 58°C. Over 500,000 years ago, giant crystals made of the mineral selenite, a type of gypsum, began to form in the cave. They have reached gigantic proportions – the largest is 4m wide and an astonishing 12m in length – almost as long as a badminton court!

Scientists in protective suits clamber over the gigantic crystals.

Opening and Closing

After water was pumped out of the cave, it was opened to scientists from 2006 until 2010. Conditions mean that explorers needed special cooling equipment and suits to investigate the cave and its extraordinary features. The crystals will deteriorate over time if left out of water, and the mining company plans to re-flood the cave with water once its work nearby is finished.

Socotra Island

This 132km-long island in the Indian Ocean lies over 240km away from Somalia and 340km from the coast of Yemen, the country to which it belongs. Isolated from mainland continents, Socotra is home to large numbers of species not found anywhere else in the world.

Isolated Island

Socotra's rugged landscape includes granite mountains, limestone caves and wide, sandy beaches. The climate is hot, dry and harsh, but living things have found ways to survive there. A United Nations biological survey in the 1990s catalogued more than 700 species only found on Socotra, including types of bats, spiders and birds, such as the Socotra cormorant. It listed more than 300 different types of trees and plants too, including the Socotran pomegranate and the cucumber tree.

A bottle tree stores water in its trunk.

The tree's giant crown, packed full of leaves, casts shade, which helps seedlings survive the hot climate.

WOW!

Sap from Socotra's Dragon's Blood trees was used in toothpastes in Europe during the eighteenth century and by Italian violin makers as a wood varnish.

Dragon's Blood

The Dragon's Blood Tree is so called for the sticky crimson sap produced in its trunk. The sap was highly-prized in the past as far back as ancient Roman times as a paint colouring, dye and as a remedy for wounds and illnesses.

The Moeraki Boulders

The small fishing village of Moeraki lies on New Zealands Otago coast around 70km north of the city of Dunedin. A short walk from Moeraki lies Koekohe Beach, from where visitors can spot seals and yellow-eyed penguins in its waters. But it's what is found on the shore that attracts the most interest – an out-of-this-world collection of mysterious ball-shaped boulders.

Layer upon Layer

Around 60 million years ago, the boulders began to form underneath layers of mud and sediment on the sea bed. Through a process called concretion, the boulders were built up from layers of sediment and minerals pressed together by the weight of the material above. The larger boulders are believed to have taken 4 million to 4.5 million years to form. They were once buried deep in cliffs made of mudstone which, over time, were eroded away to reveal these rock-like spheres.

The heaviest boulders weigh over five tonnes.

Cracking Up

The boulders have tough outer shells and a softer, partly hollow interior. Some of the boulders have calcite crystals inside them, leaving geologists scratching their heads as to how these formed. On close examination, a number of the boulders are covered in cracks called septaria, which over millions of years have been filled with quartz and other minerals.

Around two-thirds of the boulders are between 1.5m and 2.2m in diameter.

Missing Rocks

Sketches of the beach made in the 1840s and 1850s reveal far more rocks than are present today. Some, particularly the smaller boulders, were taken by treasure hunters or as souvenirs. In 1971, the New Zealand government made the site a scientific reserve to protect the boulders from further removals. It is now illegal to spray graffiti or damage them in any other way. Some of the smaller boulders taken away in the past are occasionally found on sale at online auctions.

WOW!

According to Maori legend, the boulders are gourds and baggage washed ashore from the great voyaging canoe Arai-te-uru when it was wrecked as it reached New Zealand hundreds of years ago.

Coober Pedy

In 1915, 14-year-old Willie Hutchinson, prospecting for gold with his father, discovered opal gemstones in a harsh outback region almost 850km north and inland of the Australian city of Adelaide. A mining town grew up around the area, which was originally named the Stuart Range Opal Field but later was called Coober Pedy after the Aboriginal words, 'kupa piti' meaning 'boy's waterhole'.

Opal Capital of the World

Coober Pedy and its surrounding area proved to be incredibly rich in opal deposits. So much so, that even today it produces more of the world's opals (right) than anywhere else. Opal hunters flocked from different parts of the world to live and work there. The world's largest and most valuable gem-quality opal – the Olympic Australis worth over £1.5 million – was found there in 1956.

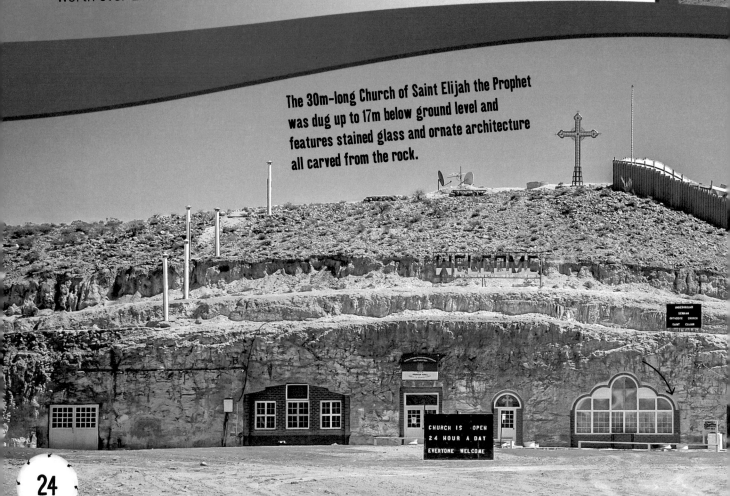

The 30m-long Church of Saint Elijah the Prophet was dug up to 17m below ground level and features stained glass and ornate architecture all carved from the rock.

CHURCH IS OPEN
24 HOUR A DAY
EVERYONE WELCOME

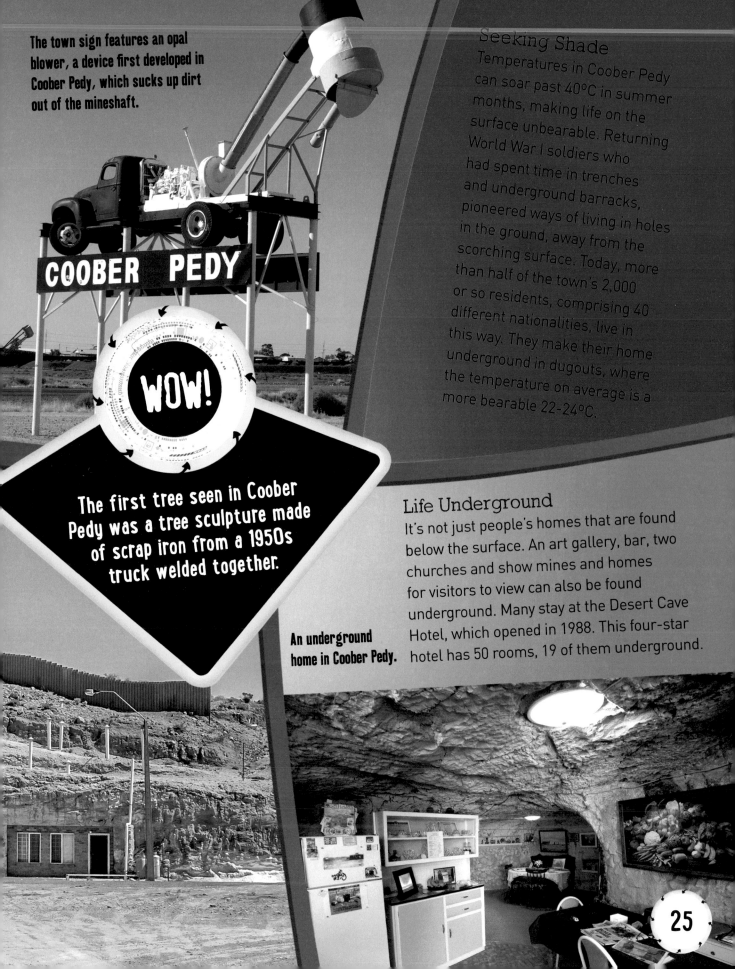

The town sign features an opal blower, a device first developed in Coober Pedy, which sucks up dirt out of the mineshaft.

COOBER PEDY

WOW!

The first tree seen in Coober Pedy was a tree sculpture made of scrap iron from a 1950s truck welded together.

Seeking Shade

Temperatures in Coober Pedy can soar past 40°C in summer months, making life on the surface unbearable. Returning World War I soldiers who had spent time in trenches and underground barracks, pioneered ways of living in holes in the ground, away from the scorching surface. Today, more than half of the town's 2,000 or so residents, comprising 40 different nationalities, live in this way. They make their home underground in dugouts, where the temperature on average is a more bearable 22-24°C.

Life Underground

It's not just people's homes that are found below the surface. An art gallery, bar, two churches and show mines and homes for visitors to view can also be found underground. Many stay at the Desert Cave Hotel, which opened in 1988. This four-star hotel has 50 rooms, 19 of them underground.

An underground home in Coober Pedy.

The Great Blue Hole

Found in a coral reef called Lighthouse Reef some 70km off the coast of the Central American nation of Belize, the Great Blue Hole is an underwater sinkhole and one of the great watery wonders of the world.

Collapsed Cave

The Blue Hole was created by a limestone cave system that started to form about 150,000 years ago. As the water level rose, the caves were flooded and its roof collapsed, making this unusual hole. It is over 300m wide and 124m deep, far deeper than the surrounding waters. It's this depth that gives the hole its distinctive dark blue colour. Small caves on its walls contain giant stalactites, some more than 7m in height.

The Great Blue Hole is fringed by coral reefs, which provide a home for a wide range of fish and marine life.

Dive, Dive, Dive!

The first scientific investigation of the Great Blue Hole was made in 1971 by the famous underwater explorer, Jacques Cousteau, and his team. Cousteau's film of the site made it famous and it became a popular dive destination. Divers have to be highly experienced and have performed at least 24 dives before they are allowed to take on the hole's dark depths. These provide habitats for anemones and some species of shark, including nurse sharks and hammerheads.

Nurse shark

WOW!

Despite being a two-hour boat ride from the coast, more than 200,000 people travel to get up close and personal with the Great Blue Hole each year.

Hammerhead sharks grow up to 6m long.

More Unusual Wonders

The unusual wonders on the previous pages are just a sample of all those found around the world. These include an upside-down forest, a fire-breathing bridge, a bright-pink lake and some seriously strange buildings.

Design Dream
The dream-like Hang Nga or Crazy House guesthouse was designed without architect's blueprints (plans). Instead the house designer, Dang Viet Nga, gave craftsmen paintings for them to follow to produce the unusual shapes and twisting structures of the building.

The fairy tale-like structures of Crazy House.

Bridge of Fire
There's a 666m-long bridge over the Han River in the Vietnamese city of Da Nang that's shaped like a dragon (left). It lights up at night via 2,500 LED lamps and even breathes fire on Saturday and Sunday nights. Awesome!

In the Pink
Found on Middle Island off the coast of Western Australia, Lake Hillier is a 600m-long, 250m-wide salty lake surrounded by a narrow strip of sand and a dense forest of eucalyptus and paperbark trees.

Brainy Building

The Lou Ruvo Center for Brain Health was opened in Las Vegas in 2010. Designed to stick in the mind by famous architect Frank Gehry, the wacky building contains 199 windows, all of which are different sizes and shapes. The entire building took 65,000 hours to engineer and includes 18,000 roof tiles all made of stainless steel.

This memorable building has four floors with patient rooms, 13 medical rooms, research labs and a museum.

The salt in the lake reacts with tiny microorganisms in the water to turn the lake a bright bubblegum-pink colour (below).

Underwater Trees

Lake Kaindy in Kazakhstan was formed in 1911 when a giant earthquake caused a large landslide. The 400m-long lake is famous for its underground forest (right) – a large collection of dead Asian Spruce tree trunks rising out of its waters.

Glossary and Further Information

cultivate
To prepare and use land to grow crops for food and materials.

endangered
A term used to describe species of living things that are under threat and may completely die out in the near future.

eroded
When landscape features such as rock or soil are worn away gradually by natural agents such as wind or flowing water.

funicular cable train
A steep railway running up the side of a cliff in which carriages are pulled up or down tracks by cables.

geologists
Scientists who study rocks and rock formations, what the Earth is made of and how it formed.

humidity
The amount of water vapour found in the air of a location at one time.

Jurassic
A period of geological time from about 200 million to 145.5 million years ago.

magma
Hot runny rock that lies underneath the Earth's crust.

meltwaters
Water formed by the melting of snow and ice, especially from a glacier.

quarrying
To cut into rock or ground in order to obtain stone or building materials.

sedimentary rock
Types of rock formed from particles and substances carried by water, ice or wind which have been pressed together over long periods of time.

sinkhole
A natural hole or depression usually caused by the collapse of a cave roof.

tonne
A unit of weight equal to 1,000 kilograms.

UNESCO
Short for the United Nations Educational, Scientific, and Cultural Organization, a part of the United Nations which helps share information and promotes projects in education and the protection of natural and man-made monuments.

Books

Visual Explorers: Wonders of the World
by Paul Calver and Toby Reynolds
(Franklin Watts, 2016)

Unpacked: Australia by Clive Gifford
(Wayland, 2014)

Discover Countries: Greece by Richard Spilsbury
(Wayland, 2013)

Websites

https://youtu.be/EEGuZRIU4RU
Get to see the Cave of Crystals in this short
documentary brought to you by the Discovery Channel.

https://theculturetrip.com/middle-east/yemen/
articles/socotra-yemens-forgotten-island/
Read an article about the island of Socotra complete
with amazing photographs.

http://www.amarcexperience.com/ui/index.
php?option=com_content&view=featured&Itemid=101
Check out precisely which aircraft have arrived, left
and are stored at the Boneyard near Tucson with this
interactive website.

http://video.nationalgeographic.com/video/australia_
cooberpedy
Watch this short video on life above and below ground
in Coober Pedy.

https://www.khanacademy.org/humanities/art-
asia/south-asia/buddhist-art2/a/the-caves-of-
ajanta
Find out more information about Ajanta's different
caves and the artistic treasures they contain at
this educational website.

http://www.amusingplanet.com/2010/08/tsingy-
stone-forest-of-madagascar.html
Check out this enticing gallery of images from the
Tsingy stone forest.

http://www.greeka.com/thessaly/meteora/
meteora-churches.htm
Learn more about the Meteora monasteries and
view photographs taken by travellers of these
extraordinary buildings.

http://www.crazyhouse.vn/index.php?lang=en
Visit the official website of the Hang Nga (Crazy
House) guesthouse in Vietnam.

http://www.boomsbeat.com/
articles/113/20140117/47-amazing-photos-salar-
de-uyuni-world-s-largest-mirrors.htm
View this amazing gallery of more than 40
photographs from the salt flats of Salar de Uyuni.

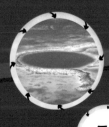

Index